hi.

i'm sorry
about the mess.

i didn't have time
to change
my life
before
you came.

i like
a sense of emptiness
about my life.

not for
anyone
else,

but for all the persons
i might become.

do you have a sense of
otherness?

yes.
i cannot describe
the oceans
between us
but i can feel their waves
washing
over
me.

you are covered
in my
nectar.

it tastes
like grapefruit.

there will be days
when
everything
is
juice
on your chin.

this is being alive.

what is happiness like?

it's like everything
you are
now
except
lighter.

you have always
been
exactly
as you are
now.

you just needed
time

to want
to be.

okay,
but like,

imagine me

10 years
from
now.

one.

i am an entity.
you
are another one.

it's okay.

there was more
room
for
me
once you left.

don't ask me
to suffer
quietly
while my life is
flooding
around me.

my spirit
was a lemon
to your parched lips.
potent.
and painful.
drawing blood from
all the cracks
you
let
thirst too long.

one.

now I love me
the way I loved you,
before you left.

i live
so
engulfed
by
my own heart.
it seems strange
you see me
as a body
at all.

i will feel better
as soon
as i remember
how to eat.

i miss the heat
radiating
of your neck
and
the soft smell
of you.

but
you keep
someone else's
feet
warm now.

one.

words
fell
across the page
like
tears
washing, gently,
against
the shores of
my heart.

imagine

if i had
spoken

the
way
i wrote.

one.

i have not been
the same

since
i read
that poem

about
eating
the plums
and not feeling sorry.

sydney boyle

fuck
what they think.

one.

you will carve
your own
path
with
the
steady
 sway
of a river
parting itself
from
the ocean.

a simple guide to success:

be honest.

what's missing?

are you the candle?
or the flame?

it doesn't matter.

they're both important.

i will never compete.
not even
with myself.

you are not
my
people
if you do not feel pulled
by
the tide
of my pulse.

your skin
tastes like salt
and
everything i was missing.

sweat
is dripping
off your chin
and
onto
my bottom lip.
your palms have soaked
through
my thin cotton skirt.
i feel the heat
conducted
between us
on
my
hip.
i want to bite you.
so i do.

find
your way
out.

one day,
you will owe
your happiness
to your decision.
to leave.

now.

today
was a little
dark.

one.

tomorrow
will
be brighter.

it was an unfortunate consequence
of existing.

i am not
for
every man.
i am woman.
for
myself.

my existence
is not an invitation
for your touch.

you didn't ask
because you knew
i would say

no.
i said no.

that
means
stop.

now!

i don't care!
get off!

press your head to my chest.
my heart
is trying
to talk.

you have always
been
more than words
to me.

wake up.

this is your life now.

one.

it's 5 a.m. on a crowded bus.
we have
calloused hands
and the moon
in
our eye.

an empty seat
beside
me
(always)
remains

empty.
even in silence
my presence
radiates
too loudly
for strangers.

i understand
the urge
to pile
on
layers
and quietly pretend
you don't exist.

it is a mistake
to think
i am just
quiet and afraid.

i am a force

bursting.

you were born
an open wound
to mistakes the world created.

you were born
capable
of
healing.

i am
pacing the floor.
waiting

for home
to feel
like home again.

your life is nothing
like mine.

you make
me
want
things

for the first time.

okay,
just imagine
my life is the same
except
it's completely different.

my words
all taste
like
tangerines.

your sweetness
is still
dripping
off
my tongue.

easy.
just pretend
it didn't
happen
and maybe

it didn't.

one.

if only
I had known
how
to be gentle
then.

i like
to take long walks
and
 forget
you ever touched me.

one.

you still smell
like peach schnapps.

i wish i could draw you a map
back
to my softness.
i could lead you to the door.
but I'm still
unsure

how to let you in.

it's okay
if you feel
a bit
disjointed.

may you learn
to bend
in new ways.

missing you
feels
like
forgetting
how
to breathe.

one.

i am
writing
my heart
back
into
my
self.

i just want
to unzip
our skins
and lie

here
for a while.

one.

i unlocked the door
and
then
he just followed
me
inside.

i'm not here to
make you
feel
important.

one.

my love
is
an inappropriate measure
of your self worth.

your love felt
like
forgiveness

for
everything
i'd ever done.

one.

be kind.

be selfish
too.

her voice
was the one
i learned
to love you with.

i hadn't
even
met
you yet.

one.

i pressed play
on that old album
and remembered
everything
as
i had left it
then.

i still feel
the
softness
of
you.

i loved you
like
i clung
to the tide.

there is no
substitute
for solitude.

there is no substitute

for the
softness

of
our fingers.
entwined

how many lives
you
have
almost lead.

how many different
people
you have already become.

you have always been an ocean.

one.

imagine
my life!
if
i had a velvet couch.

my heart
feels raw.
it must be the moon pulling
at me
agiain.

i miss
tangling
ourselves
into knots.

i'm sorry.
i can't make it to breakfast.
i'm too busy
putting
distance
between you

and
my heart.

one.

okay.
so, I hate you.

just let me
smoke.

take time for silence.
that is when
your heart speaks.

one.

i guess
this is my home
now.

please
don't forget
that you love me.

one.

i needed a break
from
investing time
in
things
that could leave.

if you want to go be
Bukowski,
go be
Bukowski.

but don't come back.

you were born
with flowers
in your mouth
and honey
in your veins.

but
you don't owe
sweetness
to anyone.

let me
set fire
to your skin
and
call it love.

one.

i want to wash
you
out
with kindness.

shush.
the women are talking.

your bartender
is not your therapist.
i know
you're lonely.
it's not their fault.

i once told you
i am turned on
by the softness
of my own
feet.

you called me
the vainest woman alive.

i still don't take it back.

yes,

i could
be trying to date.

but,
i would rather
be reading a book.

i'm in the mood
to kiss
and place a strangers hands
between
the memory of us.

we sat
side by side
(thighs touching)
and
i still felt
like i was waiting
for you to come home.

i'm sorry
i used my words to hurt you.

love
like
a hundred quiet
deaths
of who we used to be.

i am learning
to salt
my own wounds

and need
for no one.

one.

i would never barter
my love.

i plant it
tenderly
places
it was meant
to grow.

i sit beside you
quietly
and feel
the
softness
bloom
between us.

do you feel I burn
too
intensely?
i might suggest
you stand
further
back.

i refuse
to play it
cool.
i am warmth.
all
the way
through.

i wake more exhausted
than before.
my shoulders ache.

i've been trying
to reach you
across
the
bed.
you've been

drifting.

—

it's funny,
the time it takes
threading
lives together.
and the brevity of words
needed
to unravel
them again.

it took time
to be
stable
enough
to do this.

that's okay.

time is a factor
in every plan.

the thing
about
softness,
is that
it is much harder
to break.

one.

it's not my fault
you decided
not
to see me
then.

i put my fingers
to the mindless task
of loving you.

i want
you to love me.
until
my back bends
like

the
binding
of
this
book.

my heart aches
from
a backwards blood-rush.
i'm trying to retrace
steps
to a time before
my mornings knew your lips.

they're just like us
but with
less harmony
and
better sex.

you weren't trying to help.

you were waiting, watching.
hoping.
i would fail.
so you could prove
that
you knew better.

prove
that I needed you.

so we could both
pretend.

for a second.
that you deserved me.

one.

strength
is not the
ability to hide
from your feelings.

once anger failed
i was less sure what to say.

my teeth
are turning black.
i'm leaking words again.

i feel
the scratch of your cheek
against my chin
and it feels
like coming home.

pain
is
forgetting

what it is
like
to be gentle
and
remembrance

rushing back.

i spent a hundred
humid
days
gulping cheap beer
for water.

barefoot
on your dirty floors.

happy,
but aware
of the
mud
rising
between my toes.

one.

my skin
feels
like the absence
of
everything
i have ever
felt.

i spent a summer
screaming.
this is what it's like
to lose you.

nude is not a color.

it is a state
of being.

i wake up
feeling
the desert
in my bones.

it's strange
to watch your face
knowing
we
will probably end
over
all the things
i decided

weren't worth saying.

don't tie
your hope
to
someone else's dream.

you could cut
the
unforgiveness
between us.

sydney boyle

i take showers twice a day now.
peppermint scented catharsis
for
memories
of your
fingertips
wet
against my lips.
i touch my soap body
and remember
i am enough now.

be weary
of wolves
who seek
shy and quiet people.

they are looking
for the ones afraid to scream.

what do I feel like?
very lucky.

your smile
put
sunlight
back
in my bones.

it is night
and my skin
cries
for the comfort of yours.

one.

you promised
to
destroy me
but
here i am.
intact.

do not feast
on the blood of your sadness.
it cannot sustain you.

and it might just
consume
you.

the hardest part of healing
is deciding to.

take
walks.
deep breathes.

drink water.
sleep soundly.

wash your blood
clean
of unkindness.

one.

i have never
been
as
others were.

it took
time
to find my people.

i stretch myself
across the tub

and sink
beneath the steam.

lavender
lacing
through knots of my hair.

sweat
salts my lip.

the venom
of
my day
washing out.

you broke my heart
with
tenderness.

taking care
to clean
and gently wrap its pieces

so
i might rebuild it
once again.

it is

a special love
shared

between
souls

who don't need

for
one
another.

one.

creating
allows

space
for you to be

less
aware

of things ending.

imagine
if I had said no.

Made in the USA
Columbia, SC
10 July 2018